BE GOOD TO YOURSELF

george greenville butler

Green City Publishing
Austin

For Information write Green City Publishing
george butler grnciti@aol.com
Charlotte Littlefield Brown charlotte369@gmail.com
5401 S. FM 1626 170-274
Kyle, Texas 78640
(512) 772-4564

Book Cover: a beautiful painting by Laura Sikes Barrow, thanks Laura
http://laurabarrow.com/

REFLECTIONS

Today, more than ever before, certain slogans, catch phrases, etc. are being bantered about so loosely that people accept them easily without really contemplating what each means. The catch phrase," DO YOUR OWN THING" is based upon an assumption that it's perfectly right to do so, as long as doing your own thing doesn't hurt others. Today this is widely accepted. However in the act of doing your own thing, a question must be answered. Does doing your own thing hurt yourself? If the answer is yes, then clearly this would be an example of why society is in chaos and in disarray. This example illustrates the mentality that has resulted when a society is lost, doesn't have meaningful goals and is wandering from one quick fix saying to another. The divorce rate is high; child abuse, alcoholism, and drug addiction continue to plague the country.

The most alarming fact is that the family unit has disintegrated into a web of television personalities, with unrealistic desires, and falsely promulgated ambitions. Every day I meet people that remind me of television personalities. Instead of living, or developing their own individual personalities and lives, they mimic some television character that exudes zany happiness. Further the desires for goods and services are implanted so deeply within some people's minds, that it dominates their whole lives. Finally another problem is falsely promulgated ambitions, since men have put down the ladies, well it's the ladies turn to wipe their feet on such foul creatures, so they work their way to the top without family, husbands or friends, just penthouse apartments to keep them warm. With these types of personalities, desires, and ambitions no wonder nothing makes sense and few are able to live meaningful lives. All of the above trends are heightened within, the broken home where little structure is maintained so to fantasize and grab on to suggestions by others is a preoccupation.

This book has one primary goal in mind, which is to establish a perspective. One that does not interfere or replace anyone's religion, but instead helps the reader to establish an insight into his relationship with the world, while holding himself responsible for his own life. This booklet tries to portray man's true importance and relationship to the world.

Since the turn of the century there has occurred tremendous technical progress at a much faster rate than human progress, but how has this helped mankind? I am convinced that good, will come from this progress and regretfully some bad. The reason why I originated the concept of "Be Good To Yourself" is that I had a friend that was undergoing some psychological problems and as I was driving down the road one day I asked myself. What advice in as few words as possible could I give this friend that would benefit him? The answer was "Be Good to Yourself" which placed full responsibility on himself for his life and also said a hundred things about his personal psychology. The origination of the "Unified Philosophical Concept" came to me one day while drinking coffee. I started at the top of the page and wrote starting with survival the steps backward. The strength I feel of this concept is that the relationships are true either way you read them. These reflections are a primer that should be studied so that the one can better understand ones relationship to one's world, thereby establishing a foundation to build from, thus pointing oneself in a direction that one's life can take, hopefully resulting in a belief system that makes sense, ensures one's survival and helps one to:

"BE GOOD TO YOURSELF"

THE NEW GOLDEN RULE

Be Good To Yourself and Others

- george butler

BE GOOD TO YOURSELF

BE GOOD TO YOURSELF - Personal psychology

AND OTHERS - Survival rule

LOVE - Yourself equally as others

ACHIEVE - Accomplish worthwhile goals

& CREATE BEAUTY - Self Realization

FORGIVING – Release from slavery

*** BE GOOD TO YOURSELF ***

"Be Good To Yourself"

The first part of this saying "Be good to yourself" has to do with your own personal psychology and the true essence of that psychology. Within all of us we have good psychology and bad psychology; some psychologists have described this as a good side and a dark side to our personalities. The bad psychology that we carry with us is the self-defeating kind that in the end denies us happiness while the good psychology rewards ourselves and brings honor to our names. It sounds so simple "Be Good to Yourself". It sounds so simple just go out and get what you want. It is that simple but what we usually want is meaningless material things and usually these desires are insatiable desire driven. Many excellent books and techniques have been promoted as to their ability to help others. Most advocate the power of positive thinking techniques. These may be very helpful but always remember that only one person can effect real change in your life and that is yourself. It's great to have an analyst to help you but the goal of any of these techniques should be to realize or become more enlightened about yourself and the world. Religion can play a very important part in stabilizing one's life in the sense that today more than ever before people need structure that gives meaning to their lives. "Be good to Yourself" means to use every technique possible to perpetuate both your physical existence and continued spiritual growth coming out of the delusion.

"And Others"

This phrase naturally infers the "Be Good to Yourself" part which comes first. These two phrases together "Be Good To Yourself And Others" is a new and dynamic way of saying more than the "Golden Rule" remember the Golden Rule said "Do unto others as you would have them do unto you" in other words this saying means that you should be good to others and then they will be good to you. What the golden rule forgets is that man is his own worst enemy so isn't the hardest lesson in life trying to "Be Good to Yourself". Than the primary responsibility for your own goodness is yours alone, throughout history many civilizations have said the same thing in their own respective way, but now let us all assume full responsibility for our own lives

"Love"

The concept or meaning of "LOVE" used in the context of this saying is that one must strive and learn to love oneself equally as you do others. Through your good works and greater spiritual growth will you come to love yourself and the sharing of your life with another will eventually lead to an even sharing of love for yourself and others.

"Achieve"

Without accomplishment what does man have to be remembered by? It's been said dust to dust so through your work you must try and accomplish good and constructive things.

It ain't no fun being famous dust.

"And Create Beauty"

Beauty plays an important role in our lives. When we encounter beauty there follows an uplifting spiritual experience. Throughout the ages many philosophers have tried to explain and define what beauty is. Many have described beauty as good and some have used the word truth to define beauty. Aesthetics is the branch of philosophy that provides a theory of beauty. The important point is that beauty is streamed to us at the speed of light and when we experience beauty, that beauty speaks directly to our spirits, our souls, and our hearts and to each center of each atom in our bodies. This part of the saying deals with self-realization or actualization. I list it at the end for we must try and strive all of our lives to become better people, through our spiritual awakening and enlightenment. I believe and feel that when a man can leave behind beautiful works, deeds and accomplishments then and only then will he know that his life has been meaningful and worthwhile.

"Forgiving"

Forgiveness releases us from past misery – it's a cult breaker, shatters slave chains

Comments:

The saying "Be Good to Yourself" is meant as a means to live every day of your life according to the saying. Through a conscious effort to everyday conform to this way of living then will your live become more fulfilled and rewarding. Each one of us has our own individual perspectives and way of living each day. What we must do is to open ourselves to others judging them not but working with them, than our own perspective might mature, enabling us to grow and become more productive. Man enters the world frail, weak, defenseless, guilt free and open minded. Man leaves the world at an old age frail, weak, defenseless, and some guilt ridden. During our lives the guilt that each one of us carries within our own minds is always threatening. As a baby our total life experiences are in the future. Later on in life the good we do is usually quickly forgotten but the bad we do can cause us mind wrenching psychological problems. We must strive with all our might to learn how to forgive ourselves and others realizing that the responsibility for our happiness and survival lies within ourselves.

STRIVING FOR LOVE

Men find it very difficult to secure true love, instead in today's world titillation; an excited state is an unknowingly poor false substitute for real love. Man's trials and tribulations are many in his quest for love for it seems at times that as two people really fall in love there's a concerted effort by interveners to deny that good, pure, real-true love and substitute projecting on to that relationship instead their own addictions and compulsions which enslave. It's a shame but the world being not of the divine, works and operates in a worldly existing way chaining men to an earth bound realm. So it follows conversely that to be divine is to be godlike, this fallacious idea taken on by men misleads so many who are

9

striving to make sense in a seemingly unfathomable world where little sense is to found. Men must try and understand the beginnings of their slavery for their mothers who gave them life also unwittingly, unknowingly seeded into them a yearning for women's love that later can become like a drug. Men exist in an addictive-compulsive state that few men ever realize but most women by degree understand the power of granting or withholding their love, their hugs, their affections. Most men being simple minded sex-ego driven creatures never come out of that delusion that state of being, that drugged state, hypnotic, seduced little weak helpless beings stumbling around in the dark yelling "I know the way" never asking anyone for directions. Real love is non-judgmental, unconditioned and establishes within one a serenity of peace, a feeling of warmth and goodness, belonging, needing but in a non-addictive way. Love binds those together to grow one another to a higher level of understanding a new change of heart, a new direction. Forgiveness brings forth a new dawn providing god's light casting sweeping away those cobwebs of past hates, resentments and recovering, renewing that real self that existed in its pristine form shortly after our births.

There is a yearning in all of us for mama's love imprinted, bonded into us from birth but now as adults we must try and begin to love one another drawing from that child-like true love state, being like monkeys at times about the joy of loving, loving in a new way, traveling along a new path, a path of enlightenment, glory, serenity, yes a path of adventure, wanderful, wonderful even at times exciting but an excitement overshadowed by......**Real-True.....LOVE**.

Be Good To Yourself and Others,

Love, Achieve and Create Beauty

Forgiving

*** UNIFIED PHILOSOPHICAL CONCEPT ***

SUN ....The Brightest Star ... our Sun!

From the sun comes the light, nurturing life. We exist in a universe of billions of stars. The stars are scattered across billions of light years of space. It is difficult for man to imagine the vastness of space. The earliest religions were based upon sun worship with the Avant of science are Passau.

LIGHT ....The Brightest Light .. is the... Light!

LIFE ....The Brightest Life ...a worthwhile ... Life!

PERCEPTION ..The Brightest Perception..directly... into the Light!

When life first begins, perception exists. Through understanding man acquires awareness. As man's awareness increases the truth is finally realized.

AWARENESS ...The Brightest Awareness.. of...everything Present!

We being mere human being are limited in our ability to become aware of everything present so the best we can do is to expunge from ourselves the falsities and worldly conditioning that worldly influences seed into us, that inhibit us from being more fully aware of real reality.

TRUTH ...The Brightest Truth.....of all Knowledge!

	1. Realization	
Self	2. Acceptance	World
	3. Utilization	

First we must realize the truth about ourselves and the world. Secondly we must accept the truth about ourselves and the world. Thirdly we must utilize the truth about ourselves and the world. Through our utilization of the truth about ourselves and the world we begin a journey of dis-enslavement from the concepts and ideas that are man created and used to manipulate, control and enslave us to their conjured up systems of thought

SURVIVAL ... The Brightest....Survival...Creating Beauty!

We enhance our physical being so that our spiritual self might grow and prosper eventually attaining fulfillment. We attain happiness by creating beauty. Great artists and others have created art but those who have no artistic ability can prosper through the support of artists and the encouragement of others to create beautiful works of art.

FORGIVING....The Brightest...Freedom...Forgiveness of self and others

FORGIVENESS
(Integration)

The war still rages between faith and works for the way to salvation. One group the fundamentalists/evangelicals maintain that, "the way to salvation is the acceptance of Jesus Christ as your personal savior." An opposing view expressed by some main-line churches is the primary way to gain salvation is through works, the more good deeds, and greater altruistic activities that is the ticket to heaven.

The fundamentalists/evangelicals reject works as the way to salvation to heaven and instead state that those professing works are wrong while their view that acceptance of Jesus Christ as one's personal savior is the true and only way.

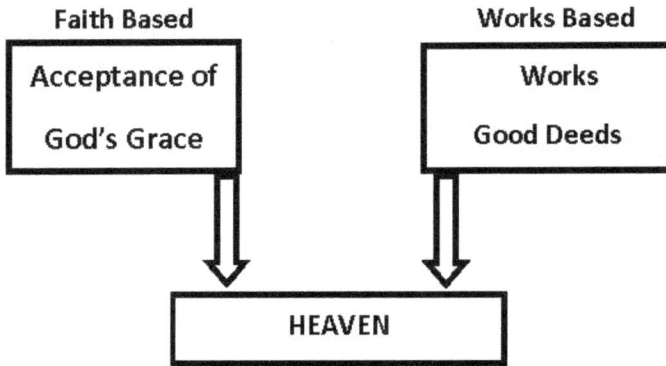

Faith Based	Works Based
Acceptance of God's Grace	Works Good Deeds

HEAVEN

My personal view is that if we truly accept God's grace and truly believe that Jesus's teachings of forgiveness is the way than that acceptance through the walking in the spirit of forgiving ourselves and others while not interfering with anyone's forgiving ways is truly walking in the spirit of God's grace. Accepting divine high minded views of God's grace and integrating it with a down to earth walking in the spirit of forgiving is truly the integration of God's grace with working to gain a metanoia sincerely trying to achieve infinitesimally a bit of God's grace on earth by acceptance and forgiving day to day.

This struggle between egos is forever ongoing no matter the subject, so to resolve this problem debating differences of religion or whatever is senseless. The problem is more fundamental and basic and is related more to the way of human nature, our emotions, and our ego state. The subjects, topics and differences in our opinions and the way we see the world are used as means to force our wills on others.

Humankind is asleep in a slumber of delusion. It is a state little realized by humankind for people are forever seeking states of comfort where the realization of true reality can be avoided and instead a fantasy of belief that is self-adulating and self-flattering is substituted. In a fantasy state we can create our own little worlds where everything is so nice and pleasing because we are all gods. The real truth is preposterous so to try and to wrap one's mind around the real truth is nearly impossible, so fantasies thrive.

FORGIVE

Forgive all always

Forgive oneself always

Forgiving ways nurture always

In The Presence of Light is Reality

That We May See, That We May Be

There are many ways to construct lying paths

but none lead to

truth

-

Perception

The intensity of our perception

and the degree of our awareness

determines the wisdom

of our will

and the worth of our

Lives

TRUTH

Truth is that which is true, correct, genuine, and real. The classical definition of truth can be discerned from Aristotle's teachings. Aristotle and other classical Greek philosophers described truth as the agreement of thought with object. This definition requires two factors, the first factor consists of a statement, belief or thought the second factor is a situation, or fact that verifies that statement, belief or thought, making it true.

The Truth exists for all to see, for all to experience, for all to be a part of. Is not the truth streamed to us from the naturally created universe? Our main dilemma is to accept or not these streams of truth. The truth is far simpler than man admits to himself, because if man accepted a simple truth than his ego would be greatly diminished and his identity would be diminished, destroying man's greatness in his own mind. Instead of accepting truth man posits and invents beliefs other than truth, disseminating this to others by all means possible. The latest and most modern high tech means are used to disseminate man's misconceptions so that these fallacies create a greater and greater confusion, disorienting and alienating man from what is.

Innate within man is truth. For the very substance of which man consists exists in reality as proof that truth is instinctually within the very existence of every atom and nucleus, these truths we define as natural laws, these are the same laws of nature that scientists study. Is it not true, that in the final analysis, matter which is wrongly indoctrinated and programmed, results in the perpetuation of untruth. Matter exists for it is in conformity with reality, so it is. Man is composed of organic matter which requires within our environment, other matter to exist. Organic matter is continuously in a state of imbalance. To insure survival this imbalance must be righted into a dynamic equilibrium through the taking in of material sustaining this organic matter. This imbalance brings about man's struggle so that inherent within man's reality is the struggle. This struggle manifests itself on the physical level by man's continuous substance gathering activities, which accomplish the furtherance of man's physical being. Man's body to continue to exist and survive must conform to its environment. It's this harsh reality that demands obedience and

20

consequences of disobedience is absolute. Ideas, thoughts, beliefs every experience that is stored and residing in man's mind is the totality of man's experience. In essence all that man is the image set library of feelings and experiences stored within man's mind. The sum total of all experiences coupled with his spiritual feelings, all taken simultaneously together, good and bad, residing within a shell of a body, is all man is.

The struggle of man is the struggle between the body and the mind; some have described it as the struggle between the physical and the spiritual. The mind is forever trying to deal with the demands of the body. Instead of always treating the body and mind as two separate entities, we must look at man in a holistic way, seeing the body and mind as differing manifestations of one dynamic (space-time). This struggle of man (wholistically) is ameliorated by wisdom which brings to man the ability to better perceive truth, resulting in, hopefully, man bringing himself into conformity with truth. The problem of man in his struggles onward is primarily how to attain truth and secondly after attaining it what to do next. To further clarify the attainment of these goals, we must first realize the truth, secondly accept the truth and thirdly utilize the truth for good.

In conclusion, in our struggle, we deny the truth about ourselves and the world, somehow thinking that this truth if admitted to ourselves threatens our survival. The very truth is what frees us, from our internal ills and the external realities of our world. Conforming to truth guarantees our existence within the light, interacting with, reflecting and emanating truth.

The good and beauty have always been related to truth.

Man because of his ego can easily come to believe he is above the physical realities of the world.

Young babies have a more simple understanding of the truth than adults, for adults have been programmed by more concepts thus are less truth filled than babies.

Truth has forever been linked with Good and Beauty. It is the harmony that truth can bring into one's life. It's important to conform to reality, to embrace truth and become enlightened.

The degree of man's perception exists on different levels of intensity.

Pursuit of truth is the pursuit of knowledge.

History has shown that when a society loses its vision and rejects the ideals of the search for truth and knowledge, it decays.

Natural Law is the moral system.

America has drifted away from the pursuit of truth and instead is pursuing an endless number of individual subjective threads, leading to and from an innumerable number of minds. This is an exercise in futility call ethical relativism or social relativism.

Truth   Absolute versus Relative

The debate between absolute truth seekers and those that believe that truth is relative has raged throughout the ages. Those that believe in absolute truth are referred in philosophical circles as absolutists and those believing that truth is relative are referred to as relativists.

The rise in the importance of science during the twentieth century has added credence to the relativists view. Heisenberg's Uncertainty Principle or sometimes referred to as The Indeterminacy Principle has been presented as proof by the relativists camp that truth is relative since matter is relative. Niles Bohr's response to Heisenberg's Principle was that of Philosophical Principle he called "complementarity" it stated that measurement of one precludes the measurement of the other. Einstein like Bohn had a more deterministic view of natural laws. Einstein believed that the Copenhagen School who supported Heisenberg's Principle to be dangerously playing with nature. Einstein believed that God doesn't play with dice.

Ilya Prigozine a Nobel Laureate believes that Quantum Mechanics proves life to be meaningless or pointless so too does Steven Weinberg author of "The First Three Minutes" as he stated in that book "The more the universe seems comprehensible, the more it (also) seems pointless". Today Heisenberg's Principle is considered to be an axiom of Physics. A friend of a friend   turned his back on his religion because of Heisenberg's

Principle. It's a crazy world when some principle posited by a physicist can shake one believes and alienate us from the universe of truth which was neither created nor established by mere physicists. There exist certain natural laws that are the same throughout the universe. These laws we describe as universal laws (meaning these laws are the same anywhere in the universe). Phenomena in our cosmos are in motion so that our cosmos is in a constant fluctuation. Some philosophers have used this fact to re enforce their view that truth is relative because of this constantly changing world. The important point is that as phenomena changes locations than the relative locations change so relativity is reality. Laws governing the makeup and appearance of matter are universal in the sense that these laws create a semblance of order in the form of a dynamic equilibrium. Thus man consists of matter obeying laws of nature but man's free will enables man to become relative in location to other phenomena. Man's ability to self-direct (ability to move) causes changes on a relativistic basis while the matter of his body is in a dynamic equilibrium with the laws of nature or natural laws.

Most matter does not have the ability to self-direct so matter that cannot self-direct itself I define as a reactive body. In nature the relativistic relationship is the space-time relationship of different phenomena.

Objective reality is that which exists outside of our mind while the reality that we experience within our minds is subjective reality. Physicists have not the power to have created the universe but only to study it.

Truth Dynamism

"The greater the communication amongst people in the absence of mind control systems, results in a greater presence of truth, as this knowledge of truth becomes more prevalent it becomes increasing more difficult for people to ignore the truth, thus resulting in more and more people acting on these truths."

--- George Butler

The following evaluation statements are to be used to help one evaluate the system of thought (World view) that one has come to accept as their belief system. Depending on the way one answers each statement determines the status of your current system of belief. Each yes answer is worth one point. A total of ten points would indicate the most worthy system. Low points on this scale of 1-10 points would indicate a system high in mind control and slavery. Pure slavery would be an example of a -0- score.

The Way?		
	Yes	No
1. The system of thought does not physically abuse, or restrain anyone in any way at any time.		
2. The system of thought does not promulgate hate, resentment or judgment.		
3. The system of thought teaches the problems of the money system constructs solutions for the money system		
4. The system of thought teaches and exposes mind control techniques practiced by all.		
5. The system of thought requires nothing from its followers.		
6. The system of thought feeds not man's ego state which continues the perpetuation of the delusion.		
7. The system of thought supports the right to defend oneself.		
8. The system of thought never interfere with anyone movement to forgiveness		
9. The system of thought never interfere with anyone's pursuit of the truth		
10. The system of thought teaches forgiveness		
Total points		

Techniques of Change - these were set out by a good friend of mine Eric Samuelson that taught me that through-out history the most subtle and dangerous change has resulted from movements that have been very slow, steady and cancerous.

1. Gradualism - has been a key technique of the Fabian Society in England that have always espoused socialism but through a steady but gradually change

2. Distraction - manifests in numerous ways primarily in the entertainment that pulls us away from the important issues of our day

3. Division - we are continually divided, pitted against one another with such all unquestioned ideas such as dualism and the Dialectic. Dualism is the idea such as good and evil, light and dark such as two independent and mutually irreducible principles or substances sometimes in conflict but at other times complimentary. The Dialectic is different from pure dualistic

thought for while dualism is stable the dialectic is a dynamic tending toward synthesis.

CULTS – the following speech was delivered to Krisnamurti's followers on August 2, 1929 before a great number of his followers meeting in Ommen, Holland. The importance of this speech is that he released his followers from cultic slavery that he finally realized all men should be free from.

Pay special attention to this story told by Krishnamurti in his speech:

"You may remember the story of how the devil and a friend of his were walking down the street, when they saw ahead of them a man stoop down and pick up something from the ground, look at it, and put it away in his pocket. The friend said to the devil, What did that man pick up? He picked up a piece of Truth, said the devil. That is a very bad business for you, then, said his friend. Oh, not at all, the devil replied, I am going to help him organize."

Krishnamurti's Speech follows:

The Dissolution of the Order of the Star

The Order of the Star in the East was founded in 1911 to proclaim the coming of the World Teacher. Krishnamurti was made Head of the Order. On August 2, 1929, the opening day of the annual Star Camp at Ommen, Holland, Krishnamurti dissolved the Order before 3000 members. Below is the full text of the talk he gave on that occasion.

"We are going to discuss this morning the dissolution of the Order of the Star. Many people will be delighted, and others will be rather sad. It is a question neither for rejoicing nor for sadness, because it is inevitable, as I am going to explain.

You may remember the story of how the devil and a friend of his were walking down the street, when they saw ahead of them a man stoop down and pick up something from the ground, look at it, and put it away in his pocket. The friend said to the devil, what did that man pick up? He picked up a piece of Truth, said the devil. That is a very bad business for you, then, said his friend. Oh, not at all, the devil replied, I am going to help him organize it.

I maintain that Truth is a pathless land, and you cannot approach it by any path whatsoever, by any religion, by any sect. That is my point of view, and I adhere to that absolutely and unconditionally. Truth, being limitless, unconditioned, unapproachable by any path whatsoever, cannot be organized; nor should any organization be formed to lead or to coerce people along any particular path. If you first understand that, then you will see how impossible it is to organize a belief. A belief is purely an individual matter, and you cannot and must not organize it. If you do, it becomes dead, crystallized; it becomes a creed, a sect, a religion, to be imposed on others. This is what everyone throughout the world is attempting to do. Truth is narrowed down and made a plaything for those who are weak, for those who are only momentarily discontented. Truth cannot be brought down, rather the individual must make the effort to ascend to it. You cannot bring the mountain-top to the valley. If you would attain to the mountain-top you must pass through the valley, climb the steeps, unafraid of the dangerous precipices.

So that is the first reason, from my point of view, why the Order of the Star should be dissolved. In spite of this, you will probably form other Orders, you will continue to belong to other organizations searching for Truth. I do not want to belong to any organization of a spiritual kind, please understand this. I would make use of an organization which would take me to London, for example; this is quite a different kind of organization, merely mechanical, like the post or the telegraph. I would use a motor car or a steamship to travel, these are only physical mechanisms which have nothing whatever to do with spirituality. Again, I maintain that no organization can lead man to spirituality.
If an organization be created for this purpose, it becomes a crutch, a weakness, a bondage, and must cripple the individual, and prevent him from growing, from establishing his uniqueness, which lies in the discovery for himself of that absolute, unconditioned Truth. So that is another reason why I have decided, as I happen to be the Head of the Order, to dissolve it. No one has persuaded me to this decision.
This is no magnificent deed, because I do not want followers, and I mean this. The moment you follow someone you cease to follow Truth. I am not concerned whether you pay attention to what I say or not. I want to do a certain thing in the world and I am going to do it with unwavering concentration. I am concerning myself with only one essential thing: to set

man free. I desire to free him from all cages, from all fears, and not to found religions, new sects, nor to establish new theories and new philosophies. Then you will naturally ask me why I go the world over, continually speaking. I will tell you for what reason I do this: not because I desire a following, not because I desire a special group of special disciples. (How men love to be different from their fellow-men, however ridiculous, absurd and trivial their distinctions may be! I do not want to encourage that absurdity.) I have no disciples, no apostles, either on earth or in the realm of spirituality.

Nor is it the lure of money, nor the desire to live a comfortable life, which attracts me. If I wanted to lead a comfortable life I would not come to a Camp or live in a damp country! I am speaking frankly because I want this settled once and for all. I do not want these childish discussions year after year.

One newspaper reporter, who interviewed me, considered it a magnificent act to dissolve an organization in which there were thousands and thousands of members. To him it was a great act because, he said: What will you do afterwards, how will you live? You will have no following, people will no longer listen to you. If there are only five people who will listen, who will live, who have their faces turned towards eternity, it will be sufficient. Of what use is it to have thousands who do not understand, who are fully embalmed in prejudice, who do not want the new, but would rather translate the new to suit their own sterile, stagnant selves? If I speak strongly, please do not misunderstand me, it is not through lack of compassion. If you go to a surgeon for an operation, is it not kindness on his part to operate even if he cause you pain? So, in like manner, if I speak straightly, it is not through lack of real affection–on the contrary.
As I have said, I have only one purpose: to make man free, to urge him towards freedom, to help him to break away from all limitations, for that alone will give him eternal happiness, will give him the unconditioned realization of the self.

Because I am free, unconditioned, whole–not the part, not the relative, but the whole Truth that is eternal–I desire those, who seek to understand me to be free; not to follow me, not to make out of me a cage which will become a religion, a sect. Rather should they be free from all fears–from the fear of religion, from the fear of salvation, from the fear of spirituality, from the fear of love, from the fear of death, from the fear of life itself. As an artist paints a picture because he takes delight in that painting, because it is his self-expression, his glory, his well-being, so I do this and not because I want anything from anyone.

You are accustomed to authority, or to the atmosphere of authority, which you think will lead you to spirituality. You think and hope that another can, by his extraordinary powers--a miracle–transport you to this realm of eternal freedom which is Happiness. Your whole outlook on life is based on that authority.

You have listened to me for three years now, without any change taking place except in the few. Now analyze what I am saying, be critical, so that you may understand thoroughly, fundamentally. When you look for an authority to lead you to spirituality, you are bound automatically to build an organization around that authority. By the very creation of that organization, which, you think, will help this authority to lead you to spirituality, you are held in a cage.

If I talk frankly, please remember that I do so, not out of harshness, not out of cruelty, not out of the enthusiasm of my purpose, but because I want you to understand what I am saying. That is the reason why you are here, and it would be a waste of time if I did not explain clearly, decisively, my point of view.

For eighteen years you have been preparing for this event, for the Coming of the World Teacher. For eighteen years you have organized, you have looked for someone who would give a new delight to your hearts and minds, who would transform your whole life, who would give you a new understanding; for someone who would raise you to a new plane of life, who would give you a new encouragement, who would set you free–and now look what is happening! Consider, reason with yourselves, and discover in what way that belief has made you different–not with the superficial difference of the wearing of a badge, which is trivial, absurd. In what manner has such a belief swept away all the unessential things of life? That is the only way to judge: in what way are you freer, greater, more dangerous to every Society which is based on the false and the unessential? In what way have the members of this organization of the Star become different?

As I said, you have been preparing for eighteen years for me. I do not care if you believe that I am the World–Teacher or not. That is of very little importance. Since you belong to the organization of the Order of the Star, you have given your sympathy, your energy, acknowledging that Krishnamurti is the World–Teacher– partially or wholly: wholly for those who are really seeking, only partially for those who are satisfied with their own half-truths.

You have been preparing for eighteen years, and look how many difficulties there are in the way of your understanding, how many complications, and how many trivial things. Your prejudices, your fears, your authorities, your churches new and old–all these, I maintain, are a barrier to understanding. I cannot make myself clearer than this. I do not want you to agree with me, I do not want you to follow me, I want you to understand what I am saying.

This understanding is necessary because your belief has not transformed you but only complicated you, and because you are not willing to face things as they are. You want to have your own gods–new gods instead of the old, new religions instead of the old, new forms instead of the old–all equally valueless, all barriers, all limitations, all crutches. Instead of old spiritual distinctions you have new spiritual distinctions, instead of old worships you have new worships. You are all depending for your spirituality on someone else, for your happiness on someone else, for your enlightenment on someone else; and although you have been preparing for me for eighteen years, when I say all these things are unnecessary, when I say that you must put them all away and look within yourselves for the enlightenment, for the glory, for the purification, and for the incorruptibility of the self, not one of you is willing to do it. There may be a few, but very, very few. So why have an organization? Why have false, hypocritical people following me, the embodiment of Truth? Please remember that I am not saying something harsh or unkind, but we have reached a situation when you must face things as they are. I said last year that I would not compromise. Very few listened to me then. This year I have made it absolutely clear. I do not know how many thousands throughout the world–members of the Order–have been preparing for me for eighteen years, and yet now they are not willing to listen unconditionally, wholly, to what I say.

As I said before, my purpose is to make men unconditionally free, for I maintain that the only spirituality is the incorruptibility of the self which is eternal, is the harmony between reason and love. This is the absolute, unconditioned Truth which is Life itself. I want therefore to set man free, rejoicing as the bird in the clear sky, unburdened, independent, ecstatic in that freedom . And I, for whom you have been preparing for eighteen years, now say that you must be free of all these things, free from your complications, your entanglements. For this you need not have an organization based on spiritual belief. Why have an organization for five or ten people in the world who understand, who are struggling, who have put aside all trivial things? And for the weak people, there can be no organization to help them to find the Truth, because Truth is in everyone; it is not far, it is not near; it is eternally there.

Organizations cannot make you free. No man from outside can make you free; nor can organized worship, nor the immolation of yourselves for a cause, make you free; nor can forming yourselves into an organization, nor throwing yourselves into works, make you free. You use a typewriter to write letters, but you do not put it on an altar and worship it. But that is what you are doing when organizations become your chief concern. How many members are there in it? That is the first question I am asked by all newspaper reporters. How many followers have you? By their number we shall judge whether what you say is true or false. I do not know how many there are. I am not concerned with that. As I said, if there were even one man who had been set free, that were enough.
Again, you have the idea that only certain people hold the key to the Kingdom of Happiness. No one holds it. No one has the authority to hold that key. That key is your own self, and in the development and the purification and in the incorruptibility of that self alone is the Kingdom of Eternity.

So you will see how absurd is the whole structure that you have built, looking for external help, depending on others for your comfort, for your happiness, for your strength. These can only be found within yourselves. You are accustomed to being told how far you have advanced, what is your spiritual status. How childish! Who but yourself can tell you if you are beautiful or ugly within? Who but yourself can tell you if you are incorruptible? You are not serious in these things. But those who really desire to understand, who are looking to find that which is eternal, without beginning and without an end, will walk together with a greater intensity, will be a danger to everything that is unessential, to unrealities, to shadows. And they will concentrate, they will become the flame, because they understand. Such a body we must create, and that is my purpose. Because of that real understanding there will be true friendship. Because of that true friendship–which you do not seem to know–there will be real cooperation on the part of each one. And this not because of authority, not because of salvation, not because of immolation for a cause, but because you really understand, and hence are capable of living in the eternal. This is a greater thing than all pleasure, than all sacrifice.

So these are some of the reasons why, after careful consideration for two years, I have made this decision. It is not from a momentary impulse. I have not been persuaded to it by anyone. I am not persuaded in such things. For two years I have been thinking about this, slowly, carefully, patiently, and I have now decided to disband the Order, as I happen to be its Head. You can form other organizations and expect someone else. With that I am not concerned, nor with creating new cages, new decorations for those cages. My only concern is to set men absolutely, unconditionally free."

When asked in 1974 by his biographer, Mary Lutyens, to define his teachings Krishnamurti wrote the following:

"The core of Krishnamurti's teaching is contained in the statement he made in 1929 when he said 'Truth is a pathless land'. Man cannot come to it through any organisation, through any creed, through any dogma, priest or ritual, not through any philosophical knowledge or psychological technique

The following example is a real-day example of institutes practicing world transformation on the public.

The Report entitled "Changing Images of Man" has a Chart entitled "Dominant Images of Humankind Throughout History" and the descriptions therein is a modern day example of the grand mechanism that the general public has been trapped into. These ideas of creating a new world-view amendable to the new age was written in this report published in 1982 entitled "Changing Images of Man" the following individuals are responsible for this publication.

"CHANGING IMAGES OF MAN"

Edited by O. W. MARKLEY
Project Director

WILLIS W. HARMAN
Project Supervisor

By the following staff of and consultants to

THE CENTER FOR THE STUDY OF
SOCIAL POLICY/SRI INTERNATIONAL:

Joseph Campbell, Duane Elgin, Willis Harman, Arthur Hastings, O. W. Markley, Floyd Matson, Brendan O'Regan and Leslie Schneider

The Stanford Research Institute has been in the forefront of behavioral research for decades so this paper born from out of this institute is no surprise, but who wants to be institutionalized by any institute.

This paper was published by Pergamon Press, enough said.

The important point to make about this paper is to study the chart found in Chapter 2 entitled "Dominant Images of Humankind Throughout History" – within this chart are preferred transformations the authors desire to be accomplished. This publication can be found on the web in pdf file format, so search and study this report and the chart and you can see the future.

NEW TRINITY

Three General World View Groups: are under the influence of the New Age Movement (NAM) also known as Cosmic Humanism (CH), NAM-CH - The New Thought Movement is a close kin to the New Age Movement. So one should also study The New Thought Movement. General World View Groups:

1. Nature Centered
2. Man Centered
3. God Centered

New Age Movement (NAM) – Cosmic Humanism (CH) is acting like a paradymical umbrella (as illustrated in the chart below) and underlying are three general world view groups that benefit from the general umbrella effect of influences of the New Age Movement NAM or Cosmic Humanism movement, NAM-CH. Below is stated that the main influence of pantheism, pan-entheism ties all major religious thought together by circumventing dogma and doctrine and appealing directly to the human and the human condition.

The Delusion is Real!

New Age Movement – Cosmic Humanism		
Pantheism – "Yea are Gods" – relates to all three world view groups overlaying them in the sense that the movement acting through the weaknesses of humankind by granting, bestowing on them godliness thus transforming them into being enslaved by false self, ego, human nature and emotions – the movement acting through weaknesses of human nature undermines the major religions of the world, reiterating the mystery school religions of the past thereby returning the world to a collective, pagan, occult based system easier to rule with neo-platonic elite-priest-gods		
False Self, Ego, Human Nature, Emotions – means of circumventing dogma and doctrines thus speaking directly to the individual stirring deluding ones state of being overriding the conscience state.		
God Centered	**Man Centered**	**Nature Centered**
Formal Religions	Atheism, Agnosticism, Secularism	Wiccan, Eastern Religions

The New Age Movement encompasses the above three general world view groups in a way of compromising the God centered view with a god-man paradigm. So The New Age Movement relates to these three general world view groups through individuals and being able to relate it surrounds and overcomes all three groups and merges them into itself into a seemingly higher consciousness state, conscience state, called the New Age Movement alias Cosmic Humanism alias Cosmic Consciousness

Today the New Age Movement, The New Thought Movement and similar Movements sell hundreds of millions of copies of their books. These successes and high sales figures do not speak well about the help the books provide but instead is an example of mass conditioning of the public into the wrong world-views that entrap them into a subservient state of thinking themselves to be gods. Replacement of the Ego problem with the God-Man problem is no solution or path to enlightenment but instead is just another false-self hustle with everyone thinking themselves to be divine. Sorry folks I am not going for that.

GOD
Forgiveness Being
Grace
Acceptance of Grace
Metanoia
"I'm Sorry
Principles to live by
There is sin
Schooled in Sprit
Light of Goodness
Awareness
Thinking

↑

Man

↓

Thoughtless
Non-aware
Light of Darkness
Schooled in Occult
There is no sin
Do your own thing
Do as thy will
I'm not Sorry
Chaos-Directionless
Confounder
Evil
Non-Forgiveness Being
Satan

Truth Has No Politics

Truth Ain't Ain't

Truth Is!

SURVIVAL

Like night and day for man there is also light and darkness. The light is represented by hope even until man's last dying breath, survival enhancement. The darkness is symbolized by death such as the last most desperate act that man can make, suicide, self-destruction. Each and every day of our lives we experience a mix of two types of activities they are:

Survival Enhancement Activities   work, exercise ton and clean living

Self-Destructive Activities   Alcoholism, drug addition, smoking and all physical and debilitating acts.

We must try and spend more of our time on survival enhancement activities and less time on self-destructive activities. Though everyday our lives are a mix of these two activities.
The chart below is another way to look at this survival issue.

Additive-Compulsive Dynamics
Two Categories:

Addiction Enabler-Facilitators	Addiction Breakers
Relativists	Absolutists
Man-Centered World viewers	God-Centered World viewers
Man Worshipers	God Worshipers
Overly compassionate	Hard Love Proponents
Modernism	Traditionalism
Secularists	Non-Secularists
Dope Pushers/ False Abstracts	Addiction Curers/ Down to Earth
Idealists	Realists
Mind Oriented	Physical Oriented
Eyes in the Sky	Feet on the Ground

THE PRIME DIRECTIVE...

To Exist!

THE DELUSION – threatens our survival

The delusion is real and is divisive for it creates chaos destroying unity, solidarity of thought solidarity of action. The powers that be are always defeating any movement that seeks to reveal the true nature of human-unkind and the existence and real essence of the hidden rule.

It's simple because we have neither the street smart or world smart to decipher the world accurately, we instead substitute imagined, conjured up reasons to fill in the blanks in forming our own world view. Trying to make sense and establishing a reasonable explanation of reality continuing to try to make sense at times of an unfathomable universe.

Delusion Problem – the delusion is synergistically driven and we all suffer from self-delusion by degree and in this state we forever seek out those imputes that support the ego state and continue this state of denial and ignorance and so most of the time the ego perpetuating delusion is the threat!.

Delusion Solution – we must strive to attain a better overall realization of the IS free from preconceptions seeded in by interpreters. To come out of the Delusion is to come out of that sleep state that overrides our true self. We must truly with a heartfelt change start walking in a state of acceptance and works, creating a dynamic through forgiving, of deriving a greater objective means of seeing reality as it IS!

The delusion arises because of the failure to accurately perceive and ascertain with good judgment the real truth of reality. So the result is a world view that is not totally accurate, true or sensible, instead we are thinking deluded thoughts and acting out on those thus separating ourselves from true reality by degree. .

C.O.O...IT

C.oming O.ut O.f...IT - a way of not being

This system of thought is meant not to be a way of being but instead is a process of release that results in a way of not being. To come out of it is to start deprogramming oneself through a real striving for truth that is unfettered with only a minimal ego system. Slavery of the mind can be accomplished through any world view whether the system is a Christian Fundamentalist or Atheistic view. They both can be wrongly used to judge. Judging results in ones thinking they have discovered some great mystery that leads toward a greater self. We all suffer from self-delusion by degree and in this state we forever seek out those imputes that support the ego state and continue the state of denial and ignorance. The ego senses wrongly that any negative about the self is a threat to the individual, a threat to ones survival. To see and accept these negatives, thus initiating a process of positive change of release is to enhance ones survival. The ego perpetuating delusion is the threat!

The following three lessons I originated are truly freeing and of real enlightenment

DIVINE LESSONS

FORGIVE ALL ALWAYS - Forgiveness releases all from a synergistic system of hate-fueled megalomaniacal creatures who manifest demagoguery of ruler ship establishing and nurturing a man created rebellion against goodness

USURY NOT - minimize interest paying thereby reducing economic slavery to those who unrightfully have gained control over the *un-natural* mechanism of money creation

DEPOSESS ALL - expunge all mind and brainwashing ideas of propaganda that govern our actions and beliefs and exorcize from all structured evil

- a former addict of lies

The ideal of *USURY NOT* - is not for man to attain such as the total elimination of usury is impossibility for man, for we exist in far specialized economic and advanced money and financial world system, so the best that can be attained is a minimization of interest paying. The less interest you pay the less you are a slave to the lender.

40

RELATIONAL PERSPECTIVE ...
.....FOR MAN !

   In the presence of light is reality. The average human life span is short
indeed so that our sun seems to have shone forever, but still underneath
this bright shining light some of us lose our way in the darkness of despair
and sadness.   One of the most important problems today is that people
have different conceptual perceptions and understandings of human
nature. The idealist thinks that everyone should be equal but it's obvious
that everyone is not equal. Some are more intelligent and talented than
others.   Man has existed on this earth for ages yet human progress has
been slow. The study of History has taught us that history repeats itself.
Perhaps from the study of history the most important lesson learned is that
we've learned nothing from the study of history. For no substantial change
has occurred in man's human nature over the ages, so that man continues
to make the same mistakes over and over creating history.   Each person
is a produce of his culture and each person creates his culture. Therefore
we must recognize destructive and decadent forces within our society
before we can change our culture for the better. These thoughts bring us
back to the same old basics.

"Know Thyself"
Oracle of Delphi

Socrates taught the above saying so that the better you know yourself, the
deeper and more realistic understanding you will achieve of your own
human weaknesses and of human nature. Using this knowledge than
should one not change oneself for the better, this awareness of human
frailties and human nature creates an enlightened self. For is it not true that
when one man has certain weaknesses and short comings than others must
also suffer from similar maladies.

Later in my thinking I added to "Know Thyself" two additional sayings.

41

KNOW THYSELF - KNOW THY THOUGHTS - KNOW THY WORLD

KNOW THYSELF

Know Thyself – was a saying used by the Greeks to teach self-knowledge. So to proactively begin to know oneself is to begin a process to better understand ones own personality and character traits so that one might be able to reform those negative traits and through experiencing a continual system of self-observation an awakening to a greater self-knowledge is attained

Psychology Personal – make use of known body of knowledge as a means to begin a foundation and paradigm that through greater knowledge and discover can be modified

Personality Analysis – enables individuals to appreciate and see the differences among themselves

Human Nature – study of the essence of human nature

Self-Awareness - is an evolving toward a means of becoming more aware of one's thoughts and seeing oneself interacting with those controlling thoughts as they unfold increasing ones self-knowledge and self-awareness attaining a heightened and elevated level of understanding.

KNOW THY THOUGHTS

Know Thy Thoughts – denotes a process of being able to observe ones thoughts as they are unfolding and come to realize how those thoughts mold one's actions. In the experiencing of one's self-observation this hopefully will become a continuous dynamic in the context of being able to observe ones thoughts as they are being processed by the mind and becoming aware of the beginning of the initiation of ones actions and later the ramifications and finally the consequences of those actions and the acceptance of being responsible for or admitting to one self the shirking of those responsibilities.

Self-Observation – the capacity of the mind to bend back upon itself, observing itself, at times this capacity is described with the terms, reflexive, reflexivity. To be able to see how these thoughts control our actions, usually very judgmental thoughts resulting in a self- re-enforcement of the ego occurs. To forgive releases us out of the ego support which frees us from mind slavery.

THE MOUNTAIN STREAM

"We are born as babes at the top of a mountain stream falling into the stream at its beginning. The stream as it sweeps down the mountainside gains a greater and greater swiftness and force. The currents grow stronger the waters swifter and deeper, throwing us hither and throe like bits of flotsam battered against the rocks engulfed by the whitewater swept just as helpless babies where the stream desires. We grow older as we progress down the stream finally able to paddle out of the center of the current seeking relief within the still waters, keeping in mind that where the stream empties into the sea there death awaits. Further down the stream we wade out of the stream standing on the hills along the shore. We stand in judgment from those hills looking down on those being swept to their deaths thinking them as fools. We must let go of this judgment replacing it with forgiveness melting our hearts, reflecting grace, vanquishing hate forever. Eventually we all relent regaining our senses and eventually rejoin the rest of humankind joining those in the stream and together ministering one to another as we are all washed to the sea, so ends our lives. The water is the light. So as our lives unfold we become inundated by an overwhelming amount of streams of light carrying conveying information, data, symbols, idols, ideas rushing into our minds fixating, molding, influencing, ruling, addicting, seducing, us. So do we not realize this or try and awaken from this slumber and accept grace reflecting the essence of that acceptance by forgiveness being, so ending the night."

KNOW THY WORLD

Know Thy World is a journey of discovery of worldly things. We should endeavor to discover those systems that control us through a systemized state of debasement. There are two levels the first is becoming *"Street Smart"* to interpersonal relationships and secondly is to try and become

"World Smart" to become aware of worldly and institutional hustles these hustles manifest in many of the following dynamics a few are freeing but the majority are enslaving.

Political System – "Physical Superiority, Orchestrating Money-Mind Sorcery" this saying describes the world system in a nutshell.

Natural Law, Social Contract, Documents – Constitution, Bill of Rights, these can be freeing

Occultism as higher control techniques – these enslave

Physics – "Time Dynamism" an earlier book I wrote in 1988 which can be attained at the University of Texas at Austin card catalog helps us establish a relational-perspective wherein ones relationship with a real physical world can be established and fully realized

History – "Historians-Storytellers", relevance of history repeating itself, revisionism

Money Secrets – teachings about fractional banking, economics – usury, Prosbul, modern economics, gold is freedom, fiat money portends destruction

Mind Control – Brain Washing, Hustles, coercive influence, DID, memory recovery

Secrets - No Secrets, No Secret Societies

New World Religion – Mammonism the new secret world religion and how it is negatively impacting a free society

Conspiracy Scholarship – goal is to educate scholars who are well informed of the real world system, every teacher a student every student a teacher

We live in a world we ourselves create

Johann Gottfried Von Herder

Johann Gottfried Von Herder was the first to posit a Religious Relativism concept. It's ironic that today this saying exudes Humanism but what kind of World has man created with a Man Centered World View. The World is not full of peace and harmony so Humanism has failed us just as man has failed us. We need more Humanitarians not Humanists.

"If only it were all so simple! If only there were evil people somewhere insidiously committing evil deeds, and it were necessary only to separate them from the rest of us and destroy them. But the line dividing good and evil cuts through the heart of every human being. And who is willing to destroy a piece of his own heart?"

— Aleksandr Solzhenitsyn, *The Gulag Archipelago 1918-1956*

"The battleline between good and evil runs through the heart of every man."

Aleksandr Solzhenitsyn

So in the end we need to strive to overcome and save ourselves from ourselves.

DESTINY

Eventually each one of us finally realizes that we are alone with our destiny. Each man must assume responsibility for his own life, yes for his own destiny.

Each Man is Alone

With his

Destiny.

Man's very nature can be aggressive and overwhelming at times, but does this not demonstrate the very characteristics that have enabled man to survive this long. Yes the emotional aspect of man has and does create problems but man's ability to reason and overcome his problems coupled with his instincts have resulted in man's continued survival.

SELF HELP

These saying should be recited before bedtime and after arising each morning.

1. I will forgive myself and others for the past!

2. I will always seek the truth!

3. I will never interfere with truth seeking!

4. I will utilize the truth for good!

SOCIAL SYNERGY

From Birth – In the beginning at birth I believe we are as close to our real core self as we'll ever be. Almost immediately our parents begin to condition us and thus they induce into us the burdens, shortcomings and weaknesses that they suffer. So a new born babe cannot escape this state. I believe that a Multiple Personality Disorder dynamic occurs, some might describe as naturally occurring. Neither the parents nor the babe realize that this unfolding dynamic is occurring. Creation and growing of a false self begins from out of this dynamic. Today MPD (Multiple Personality Disorder) has been renamed to DID (Dissociative Identity Disorder).

The Man Problem – In my early thinking I begin to realize the problems of the world that can be attributed to men. In my opinion I would say that about 80% of the world's problems can be attributed to men. Women are life givers and life nurtures while men seem to be more ego driven. Men such as Charles Dickens with their creative energies have made great contributions to the world. Than can we concluded that the strength of men rests with their ability to think in the abstract and create great works of art, benefiting the world. Adversely so men's ability to think in the abstract can also mean that men can glob upon more wrong headed ideas to support their egos than women. Extrapolating out this thought can lead to men thinking themselves to be gods, so too do women but by a lesser degree. Men must begin to manage their egos instead of letting their egos manage and dominate them.

Delusion – I speak about delusion in this book and use the definition that for one to become deluded is to be educated, conditioned, and mesmerized into a deluded state with false, wrong, inaccurate information and knowledge. In this ill-informed, ignorant state we can be easily controlled and manipulated by others.

Insight - The following two paragraphs were secured from the Wikipedia which has become an authority of sorts but which influences millions if not billions daily so if the definitions are a reflection of widely accepted teaching practices than the information can function to delude the public.

A **delusion** is a <u>belief</u> held with strong conviction despite superior evidence to the contrary.[1] As a pathology, it is distinct from a belief based on false or incomplete information, <u>confabulation</u>, <u>dogma</u>, <u>illusion</u>, or other effects of <u>perception</u>........Wikipedia

Delusions typically occur in the context of neurological or <u>mental illness,</u> although they are not tied to any particular disease and have been found to occur in the context of many pathological states (both physical and mental). However, they are of particular diagnostic importance in <u>psychotic</u> disorders including <u>schizophrenia</u>, <u>paraphrenia</u>, <u>manic</u> episodes of <u>bipolar disorder</u>, and <u>psychotic depression</u>............Wikipedia

My definition of Delusion is one that states that yes it is a result of false and incomplete information being feed into us so as to attain easily manipulated deluded fools which the elites can easily control. To delude as defined by Meriam-Webster is:

> 1 **:** to mislead the mind or judgment of **:** <u>deceive</u>, <u>trick</u>....Meriam-Webster

So the public has been deluded through deceit and trickery by elitists to effectively control them.

The following rewriting of the above definition **A Delusion** hopefully provides us insight into the real state that we all exist. Earlier I have tried to define delusion but when one substitutes for **Delusion – Our Concept of Reality......**defined as the most generally held view of our reality by the greatest number of people, than one can see that **Our Concept of Reality is intentionally deluded to establish a control mechanism of us sheep. We is ill....ill informed.....ill educated.....ill of being....... street smart, ill of being.....world smart.......just a bunch of no-bodies..........ignoramuses.**

Our Concept of Reality is actually a (virtually reality) created between the interaction of a dominant elite taking advantage of a human nature that in a cultural setting primarily generates transgressions among its peoples, so non forgiving ways is an inner self-directed slave state, sort of a failed

48

inner state of affairs that manifests in outward physical reality in the public world.

The following two paragraphs are an example of my rewriting of the new mind-wash concepts, the new mind-wash way of controlling the public at large. I hopefully am revealing a greater insightful truth of these techniques.

Our Concept of Reality is a belief held with strong conviction despite hidden, suppressed evidence to the contrary.[1] As a pathology, it is not distinct from a belief based on false or incomplete information, confabulation, dogma, illusion, or other effects of perception.

Our Concept of Reality typically occurs in the context of neurological or mental illness, although it is not tied to any particular disease and has been found to occur in the context of many pathological states (both physical and mental). However, it is of particular diagnostically important in psychotic disorders including schizophrenia, paraphrenia, manic episodes of bipolar disorder, and psychotic depression.

The Concept of Reality – as used in the context above is the most widely held concept that most people accept as true reality.

Some worldview theorists postulate that so called psychopaths who rule the world have intentionally and unintentionally induced into the population at large a mental illness. This is aided by a system of crony, monopolistic; Babylonian Capitalism that synergistically with other factors builds a false reality that is passed off to the public at large as true reality. The higher education system functions to re-enforce this system of false (true reality) inducing a mental illness one can define as: well educated programmed individuals.

Coming Home

I watched recently one spring a flock of geese as I was viewing them from out of a department store window. They were flying from west to east then took a left turn headed north. The homing instinct is very strong and geese have a very powerful visual look see to enable them to return to their summer grounds which are in Canada.

We too as humans have a powerful homing instinct that returns us to our true self our real conscious-conscience state if left alone to operate. The enculturation of humans begins at birth and I maintain that this delusional ego state created prevents us from being able to see ourselves.

The Delusion hides The Delusion

We must throw off these culture chains and begin walking in the spirit of forgiveness which enables us to return to that real self and return to the real conscience state. Psychopaths have no conscience that is an all the more important fact that returning to the conscience, a centering, righting and goodness mechanism enables us to attain a serenity of peace and happiness, so we no longer need to feed the ego with hate or resentment but instead live in the serenity of the forgiving moment.

Synergy – We exist in a field of light and energy. Within this field we are continuously being inundated by light, streams of light. I define a stream of light containing a good idea but adversely so a stream of light may contain a light of darkness an idea that creates confusion, perpetuates a state of ignorance, division and nurtures confounding dynamics. In a state of confusion we fail to see ourselves thus "The Delusion Hides the Delusion" in this state I believe that to begin to walk in the spirit of forgiveness we can begin to become more objective and begin to see ourselves in our fallen state, the false self feels threatened and will resist with all its might to deny the truth to itself thus to the individual for its very existence is threatened and so it is. When we can truly begin to forgive ourselves and others we will begin to truly become free from cults, rituals, groups and organizations that control us. Thus to forgive is to cult break. To come out of a state of confoundment to a state of enlightenment should be our goal and the path to knowing oneself begins with forgiving oneself and others.

ENLIGHTENMENT ≠ CONFOUNDMENT

FORGIVENESS = FREEDOM

RECOVERING THE CONSCIENCE STATE

Conscious State and the Conscience State – the "Conscious State is physically driven and the "Conscience State" is mind, heart and soul driven. One is physically nurtured and the other spiritually nurtured.

Many supporters of eastern views cast aside the ego, and state that some new energy takes up residence – dwelling in them, the power of the moment, my view is simpler, it establishes a greater objectivity through forgiving and my view is neither cult of personality captured nor cult captured and I believe is clearer.

Our consciences have been overwhelmed by relativism do you think that there are no sins "Ye Are Gods" – Gods can't sin are you kidding me……..…but men can sin that's for sure.

Human nature is thus sin receptive which results from man's inability to know oneself and one's refusal to not act sinfully. Social and Moral Relativism just allows people to excuse their reckless and sinful behavior.

CONCLUSION

Have you ever felt lost in what seems at times a senseless and cruel world? Sometimes life does seem hopeless, but there is hope, like the hope a new born child brings into the world, with a clear, perceptive and beautiful mind, struggling to survive with honesty. Unlike a new born child, as our lives progress we seem to become less honest with ourselves and our psychology becomes muddled, less clear, accumulating cobwebs of guilt for the shame we brought ourselves. Perhaps the answer is closer than you think for no matter how much help you receive, isn't real change finally initiated from within your own mind and most importantly from within our hearts. We exist in a world where we live and die and as a result of this dilemma the greatest drive we have is to survive, though at times our self-destructive tendencies seem to overwhelm us, still deep down we want to love, prosper, and achieve a fulfilling life. How do we find happiness? You achieve happiness by learning how to:

"BE GOOD TO YOURSELF AND OTHERS"…..

GLOSSARY

Decision-making, belief, and behavioral biases – this list was secured from Wikipedia Commons – No changes were made to this list and all notes were included to indicate sources. See http://creativecommons.org/licenses/by-sa/3.0/

This list illustrates how easily we can mislead ourselves, so this list is provided in Glossary form to be used as a tool to help one come out of the delusion created from birth that later is so much, self-imposed.

Many of these biases affect belief formation, business and economic decisions, and human behavior in general. They arise as a replicable result to a specific condition: when confronted with a specific situation, the deviation from what is normally expected can be characterized by:

Name	Description
Ambiguity effect	The tendency to avoid options for which missing information makes the probability seem "unknown."[8]
Anchoring or focalism	The tendency to rely too heavily, or "anchor," on one trait or piece of information when making decisions (usually the first piece of information that we acquire on that subject)[9][10]
Attentional bias	The tendency of our perception to be affected by our recurring thoughts.[11]
Availability heuristic	The tendency to overestimate the likelihood of events with greater "availability" in memory, which can be influenced by how recent the memories are or how unusual or emotionally charged they may be.[12]
Availability	A self-reinforcing process in which a collective belief

cascade	gains more and more plausibility through its increasing repetition in public discourse (or "repeat something long enough and it will become true").[13]
Backfire effect	When people react to disconfirming evidence by strengthening their beliefs.[14]
Bandwagon effect	The tendency to do (or believe) things because many other people do (or believe) the same. Related to groupthink and herd behavior.[15]
Base rate fallacy or **base rate neglect**	The tendency to ignore base rate information (generic, general information) and focus on specific information (information only pertaining to a certain case).[16]
Belief bias	An effect where someone's evaluation of the logical strength of an argument is biased by the believability of the conclusion.[17]
Bias blind spot	The tendency to see oneself as less biased than other people, or to be able to identify more cognitive biases in others than in oneself.[18]
Cheerleader effect	The tendency for people to appear more attractive in a group than in isolation.[19]
Choice-supportive bias	The tendency to remember one's choices as better than they actually were.[20]
Clustering illusion	The tendency to overestimate the importance of small runs, streaks, or clusters in large samples of random data (that is, seeing phantom patterns).[10]
Confirmation bias	The tendency to search for, interpret, focus on and remember information in a way that confirms one's preconceptions.[21]

Congruence bias	The tendency to test hypotheses exclusively through direct testing, instead of testing possible alternative hypotheses.[10]
Conjunction fallacy	The tendency to assume that specific conditions are more probable than general ones.[22]
Conservatism or **regressive bias**	A certain state of mind wherein high values and high likelihoods are overestimated while low values and low likelihoods are underestimated.[23][24][25][*unreliable source?*]
Conservatism (Bayesian)	The tendency to revise one's belief insufficiently when presented with new evidence.[23][26][27]
Contrast effect	The enhancement or reduction of a certain perception's stimuli when compared with a recently observed, contrasting object.[28]
Curse of knowledge	When better-informed people find it extremely difficult to think about problems from the perspective of lesser-informed people.[29]
Decoy effect	Preferences for either option A or B changes in favor of option B when option C is presented, which is similar to option B but in no way better.
Denomination effect	The tendency to spend more money when it is denominated in small amounts (e.g. coins) rather than large amounts (e.g. bills).[30]
Distinction bias	The tendency to view two options as more dissimilar when evaluating them simultaneously than when evaluating them separately.[31]
Duration neglect	The neglect of the duration of an episode in determining its value

Empathy gap	The tendency to underestimate the influence or strength of feelings, in either oneself or others.
Endowment effect	The fact that people often demand much more to give up an object than they would be willing to pay to acquire it.[32]
Essentialism	Categorizing people and things according to their essential nature, in spite of variations.[dubious – discuss][33]
Exaggerated expectation	Based on the estimates, real-world evidence turns out to be less extreme than our expectations (conditionally inverse of the conservatism bias).[unreliable source?][23][34]
Experimenter's or expectation bias	The tendency for experimenters to believe, certify, and publish data that agree with their expectations for the outcome of an experiment, and to disbelieve, discard, or downgrade the corresponding weightings for data that appear to conflict with those expectations.[35]
Focusing effect	The tendency to place too much importance on one aspect of an event.[36]
Forer effect or Barnum effect	The observation that individuals will give high accuracy ratings to descriptions of their personality that supposedly is tailored specifically for them, but are in fact vague and general enough to apply to a wide range of people. This effect can provide a partial explanation for the widespread acceptance of some beliefs and practices, such as astrology, fortune telling, graphology, and some types of personality tests.
Framing effect	Drawing different conclusions from the same information, depending on how or by whom that information is presented.

Frequency illusion	The illusion in which a word, a name or other thing that has recently come to one's attention suddenly seems to appear with improbable frequency shortly afterwards (see also recency illusion).[37] Colloquially, this illusion is known as the Baader-Meinhof Phenomenon.[38]
Functional fixedness	Limits a person to using an object only in the way it is traditionally used.
Gambler's fallacy	The tendency to think that future probabilities are altered by past events, when in reality they are unchanged. Results from an erroneous conceptualization of the law of large numbers. For example, "I've flipped heads with this coin five times consecutively, so the chance of tails coming out on the sixth flip is much greater than heads."
Hard–easy effect	Based on a specific level of task difficulty, the confidence in judgments is too conservative and not extreme enough[23][39][40][41]
Hindsight bias	Sometimes called the "I-knew-it-all-along" effect, the tendency to see past events as being predictable[42] at the time those events happened.
Hostile media effect	The tendency to see a media report as being biased, owing to one's own strong partisan views.
Hot-hand fallacy	The "hot-hand fallacy" (also known as the "hot hand phenomenon" or "hot hand") is the fallacious belief that a person who has experienced success has a greater chance of further success in additional attempts.
Hyperbolic discounting	Discounting is the tendency for people to have a stronger preference for more immediate payoffs relative to later payoffs. Hyperbolic discounting leads

to choices that are inconsistent over time – people make choices today that their future selves would prefer not to have made, despite using the same reasoning.[43] Also known as current moment bias, present-bias, and related to Dynamic inconsistency.

Identifiable victim effect	The tendency to respond more strongly to a single identified person at risk than to a large group of people at risk.[44]
IKEA effect	The tendency for people to place a disproportionately high value on objects that they partially assembled themselves, such as furniture from IKEA, regardless of the quality of the end result.
Illusion of control	The tendency to overestimate one's degree of influence over other external events.[45]
Illusion of validity	Belief that furtherly acquired information generates additional relevant data for predictions, even when it evidently does not.[46]
Illusory correlation	Inaccurately perceiving a relationship between two unrelated events.[47][48]
Impact bias	The tendency to overestimate the length or the intensity of the impact of future feeling states.[49]
Information bias	The tendency to seek information even when it cannot affect action.[50]
Insensitivity to sample size	The tendency to under-expect variation in small samples
Irrational escalation	The phenomenon where people justify increased investment in a decision, based on the cumulative prior

investment, despite new evidence suggesting that the decision was probably wrong. Also known as the sunk cost fallacy.

Less-is-better effect	The tendency to prefer a smaller set to a larger set judged separately, but not jointly
Loss aversion	"the disutility of giving up an object is greater than the utility associated with acquiring it".[51] (see also Sunk cost effects and endowment effect).
Mere exposure effect	The tendency to express undue liking for things merely because of familiarity with them.[52]
Money illusion	The tendency to concentrate on the nominal value (face value) of money rather than its value in terms of purchasing power.[53]
Moral credential effect	The tendency of a track record of non-prejudice to increase subsequent prejudice.
Negativity effect	The tendency of people, when evaluating the causes of the behaviors of a person they dislike, to attribute their positive behaviors to the environment and their negative behaviors to the person's inherent nature.
Negativity bias	Psychological phenomenon by which humans have a greater recall of unpleasant memories compared with positive memories.[54]
Neglect of probability	The tendency to completely disregard probability when making a decision under uncertainty.[55]
Normalcy bias	The refusal to plan for, or react to, a disaster which has never happened before.

Not invented here	Aversion to contact with or use of products, research, standards, or knowledge developed outside a group. Related to IKEA effect.
Observation selection bias	The effect of suddenly noticing things that were not noticed previously – and as a result wrongly assuming that the frequency has increased.
Observer-expectancy effect	When a researcher expects a given result and therefore unconsciously manipulates an experiment or misinterprets data in order to find it (see also subject-expectancy effect).
Omission bias	The tendency to judge harmful actions as worse, or less moral, than equally harmful omissions (inactions).[56]
Optimism bias	The tendency to be over-optimistic, overestimating favorable and pleasing outcomes (see also wishful thinking, valence effect, positive outcome bias).[57][58]
Ostrich effect	Ignoring an obvious (negative) situation.
Outcome bias	The tendency to judge a decision by its eventual outcome instead of based on the quality of the decision at the time it was made.
Overconfidence effect	Excessive confidence in one's own answers to questions. For example, for certain types of questions, answers that people rate as "99% certain" turn out to be wrong 40% of the time.[23][59][60][61]
Pareidolia	A vague and random stimulus (often an image or sound) is perceived as significant, e.g., seeing images of animals or faces in clouds, the man in the moon, and hearing non-existent hidden messages on records played in reverse.

Pessimism bias	The tendency for some people, especially those suffering from depression, to overestimate the likelihood of negative things happening to them.
Planning fallacy	The tendency to underestimate task-completion times.[49]
Post-purchase rationalization	The tendency to persuade oneself through rational argument that a purchase was a good value.
Pro-innovation bias	The tendency to have an excessive optimism towards an invention or innovation's usefulness throughout society, while often failing to identify its limitations and weaknesses.
Pseudocertainty effect	The tendency to make risk-averse choices if the expected outcome is positive, but make risk-seeking choices to avoid negative outcomes.[62]
Reactance	The urge to do the opposite of what someone wants you to do out of a need to resist a perceived attempt to constrain your freedom of choice (see also Reverse psychology).
Reactive devaluation	Devaluing proposals only because they are purportedly originated with an adversary.
Recency illusion	The illusion that a word or language usage is a recent innovation when it is in fact long-established (see also frequency illusion).
Restraint bias	The tendency to overestimate one's ability to show restraint in the face of temptation.
Rhyme as reason effect	Rhyming statements are perceived as more truthful. A famous example being used in the O.J Simpson trial

with the defense's use of the phrase "If the gloves don't fit, then you must acquit."

Risk compensation / Peltzman effect	The tendency to take greater risks when perceived safety increases.
Selective perception	The tendency for expectations to affect perception.
Semmelweis reflex	The tendency to reject new evidence that contradicts a paradigm.[27]
Social comparison bias	The tendency, when making hiring decisions, to favour potential candidates who don't compete with one's own particular strengths.[63]
Social desirability bias	The tendency to over-report socially desirable characteristics or behaviours in one self and under-report socially undesirable characteristics or behaviours.[64]
Status quo bias	The tendency to like things to stay relatively the same (see also loss aversion, endowment effect, and system justification).[65][66]
Stereotyping	Expecting a member of a group to have certain characteristics without having actual information about that individual.
Subadditivity effect	The tendency to judge probability of the whole to be less than the probabilities of the parts.[67]
Subjective validation	Perception that something is true if a subject's belief demands it to be true. Also assigns perceived connections between coincidences.

Survivorship bias	Concentrating on the people or things that "survived" some process and inadvertently overlooking those that didn't because of their lack of visibility.
Time-saving bias	Underestimations of the time that could be saved (or lost) when increasing (or decreasing) from a relatively low speed and overestimations of the time that could be saved (or lost) when increasing (or decreasing) from a relatively high speed.
Unit bias	The tendency to want to finish a given unit of a task or an item. Strong effects on the consumption of food in particular.[68]
Well travelled road effect	Underestimation of the duration taken to traverse oft-traveled routes and overestimation of the duration taken to traverse less familiar routes.
Zero-risk bias	Preference for reducing a small risk to zero over a greater reduction in a larger risk.
Zero-sum heuristic	Intuitively judging a situation to be zero-sum (i.e., that gains and losses are correlated). Derives from the zero-sum game in game theory, where wins and losses sum to zero.[69][70] The frequency with which this bias occurs may be related to the social dominance orientation personality factor.

Social biases

Most of these biases are labeled as attributional biases.

Name	Description
Actor–observer bias	The tendency for explanations of other individuals' behaviors to overemphasize the influence of their personality and underemphasize the influence of their

situation (see also Fundamental attribution error), and for explanations of one's own behaviors to do the opposite (that is, to overemphasize the influence of our situation and underemphasize the influence of our own personality).

Defensive attribution hypothesis	Attributing more blame to a harm-doer as the outcome becomes more severe or as personal or situational similarity to the victim increases.
Dunning–Kruger effect	An effect in which incompetent people fail to realise they are incompetent because they lack the skill to distinguish between competence and incompetence. Actual competence may weaken self-confidence, as competent individuals may falsely assume that others have an equivalent understanding.[71]
Egocentric bias	Occurs when people claim more responsibility for themselves for the results of a joint action than an outside observer would credit them.
Extrinsic incentives bias	An exception to the *fundamental attribution error*, when people view others as having (situational) extrinsic motivations and (dispositional) intrinsic motivations for oneself
False consensus effect	The tendency for people to overestimate the degree to which others agree with them.[72]
Forer effect (aka Barnum effect)	The tendency to give high accuracy ratings to descriptions of their personality that supposedly are tailored specifically for them, but are in fact vague and general enough to apply to a wide range of people. For example, horoscopes.
Fundamental	The tendency for people to over-emphasize personality-

attribution error	based explanations for behaviors observed in others while under-emphasizing the role and power of situational influences on the same behavior (see also actor-observer bias, group attribution error, positivity effect, and negativity effect).[73]
Group attribution error	The biased belief that the characteristics of an individual group member are reflective of the group as a whole or the tendency to assume that group decision outcomes reflect the preferences of group members, even when information is available that clearly suggests otherwise.
Halo effect	The tendency for a person's positive or negative traits to "spill over" from one personality area to another in others' perceptions of them (see also physical attractiveness stereotype).[74]
Illusion of asymmetric insight	People perceive their knowledge of their peers to surpass their peers' knowledge of them.[75]
Illusion of external agency	When people view self-generated preferences as instead being caused by insightful, effective and benevolent agents
Illusion of transparency	People overestimate others' ability to know them, and they also overestimate their ability to know others.
Illusory superiority	Overestimating one's desirable qualities, and underestimating undesirable qualities, relative to other people. (Also known as "Lake Wobegon effect," "better-than-average effect," or "superiority bias").[76]
Ingroup bias	The tendency for people to give preferential treatment to others they perceive to be members of their own groups.

Just-world hypothesis	The tendency for people to want to believe that the world is fundamentally just, causing them to rationalize an otherwise inexplicable injustice as deserved by the victim(s).
Moral luck	The tendency for people to ascribe greater or lesser moral standing based on the outcome of an event
Naïve cynicism	Expecting more *egocentric bias* in others than in oneself
Naïve realism	The belief that we see reality as it really is – objectively and without bias; that the facts are plain for all to see; that rational people will agree with us; and that those who don't are either uninformed, lazy, irrational, or biased.
Outgroup homogeneity bias	Individuals see members of their own group as being relatively more varied than members of other groups.[77]
Projection bias	The tendency to unconsciously assume that others (or one's future selves) share one's current emotional states, thoughts and values.[78]
Self-serving bias	The tendency to claim more responsibility for successes than failures. It may also manifest itself as a tendency for people to evaluate ambiguous information in a way beneficial to their interests (see also group-serving bias).[79]
Shared information bias	Known as the tendency for group members to spend more time and energy discussing information that all members are already familiar with (i.e., shared information), and less time and energy discussing information that only some members are aware of (i.e., unshared information).[80]

System justification	The tendency to defend and bolster the status quo. Existing social, economic, and political arrangements tend to be preferred, and alternatives disparaged sometimes even at the expense of individual and collective self-interest. (See also status quo bias.)
Trait ascription bias	The tendency for people to view themselves as relatively variable in terms of personality, behavior, and mood while viewing others as much more predictable.
Ultimate attribution error	Similar to the fundamental attribution error, in this error a person is likely to make an internal attribution to an entire group instead of the individuals within the group.
Worse-than-average effect	A tendency to believe ourselves to be worse than others at tasks which are difficult[81]

Memory errors and biases

Main article: List of memory biases

In psychology *and* cognitive science, a **memory bias** is a cognitive bias that either enhances or impairs the recall of a memory (either the chances that the memory will be recalled at all, or the amount of time it takes for it to be recalled, or both), or that alters the content of a reported memory. There are many types of memory bias, including:

Name	Description
Bizarreness effect	Bizarre material is better remembered than common material.
Choice-supportive bias	In a self-justifying manner retroactively ascribing one's choices to be more informed than they were when they were made.

Change bias	After an investment of effort in producing change, remembering one's past performance as more difficult than it actually was[82][*unreliable source?*]
<u>Childhood amnesia</u>	The retention of few memories from before the age of four.
Conservatism or **Regressive bias**	Tendency to remember high values and high likelihoods/probabilities/frequencies lower than they actually were and low ones higher than they actually were. Based on the evidence, memories are not extreme enough[24][25]
Consistency bias	Incorrectly remembering one's past attitudes and behaviour as resembling present attitudes and behaviour.[83]
<u>Context effect</u>	That cognition and memory are dependent on context, such that out-of-context memories are more difficult to retrieve than in-context memories (e.g., recall time and accuracy for a work-related memory will be lower at home, and vice versa)
<u>Cross-race effect</u>	The tendency for people of one race to have difficulty identifying members of a race other than their own.
<u>Cryptomnesia</u>	A form of *misattribution* where a memory is mistaken for imagination, because there is no subjective experience of it being a memory.[82]
<u>Egocentric bias</u>	Recalling the past in a self-serving manner, e.g., remembering one's exam grades as being better than they were, or remembering a caught fish as bigger than it really was.
<u>Fading affect bias</u>	A bias in which the emotion associated with

unpleasant memories fades more quickly than the emotion associated with positive events.[84]

False memory	A form of *misattribution* where imagination is mistaken for a memory.
Generation effect (Self-generation effect)	That self-generated information is remembered best. For instance, people are better able to recall memories of statements that they have generated than similar statements generated by others.
Google effect	The tendency to forget information that can be found readily online by using Internet search engines.
Hindsight bias	The inclination to see past events as being more predictable than they actually were; also called the "I-knew-it-all-along" effect.
Humor effect	That humorous items are more easily remembered than non-humorous ones, which might be explained by the distinctiveness of humor, the increased cognitive processing time to understand the humor, or the emotional arousal caused by the humor.[*citation needed*]
Illusion of truth effect	That people are more likely to identify as true statements those they have previously heard (even if they cannot consciously remember having heard them), regardless of the actual validity of the statement. In other words, a person is more likely to believe a familiar statement than an unfamiliar one.
Illusory correlation	Inaccurately remembering a relationship between two events.[23][48]
Lag effect	See spacing effect.

Leveling and Sharpening	Memory distortions introduced by the loss of details in a recollection over time, often concurrent with sharpening or selective recollection of certain details that take on exaggerated significance in relation to the details or aspects of the experience lost through leveling. Both biases may be reinforced over time, and by repeated recollection or re-telling of a memory.[85]
Levels-of-processing effect	That different methods of encoding information into memory have different levels of effectiveness.[86]
List-length effect	A smaller percentage of items are remembered in a longer list, but as the length of the list increases, the absolute number of items remembered increases as well.[87][*further explanation needed*]
Misinformation effect	Memory becoming less accurate because of interference from *post-event information*.[88]
Modality effect	That memory recall is higher for the last items of a list when the list items were received via speech than when they were received through writing.
Mood-congruent memory bias	The improved recall of information congruent with one's current mood.
Next-in-line effect	That a person in a group has diminished recall for the words of others who spoke immediately before himself, if they take turns speaking.[89]
Part-list cueing effect	That being shown some items from a list and later retrieving one item causes it to become harder to retrieve the other items[90]
Peak–end rule	That people seem to perceive not the sum of an experience but the average of how it was at its peak

(e.g. pleasant or unpleasant) and how it ended.

Persistence
The unwanted recurrence of memories of a traumatic event.[*citation needed*]

Picture superiority effect
The notion that concepts that are learned by viewing pictures are more easily and frequently recalled than are concepts that are learned by viewing their written word form counterparts.[91][92][93][94][95][96]

Positivity effect
That older adults favor positive over negative information in their memories.

Primacy effect, Recency effect & Serial position effect
That items near the end of a sequence are the easiest to recall, followed by the items at the beginning of a sequence; items in the middle are the least likely to be remembered.[97]

Processing difficulty effect
That information that takes longer to read and is thought about more (processed with more difficulty) is more easily remembered.[98]

Reminiscence bump
The recalling of more personal events from adolescence and early adulthood than personal events from other lifetime periods[99]

Rosy retrospection
The remembering of the past as having been better than it really was.

Self-relevance effect
That memories relating to the self are better recalled than similar information relating to others.

Source confusion
Confusing episodic memories with other information, creating distorted memories.[100]

Spacing effect
That information is better recalled if exposure to it is repeated over a long span of time rather than a short

one.

Spotlight effect	The tendency to overestimate the amount that other people notice your appearance or behavior.
Stereotypical bias	Memory distorted towards stereotypes (e.g., racial or gender), e.g., "black-sounding" names being misremembered as names of criminals.[82][*unreliable source?*]
Suffix effect	Diminishment of the recency effect because a sound item is appended to the list that the subject is *not* required to recall.[101][102]
Suggestibility	A form of misattribution where ideas suggested by a questioner are mistaken for memory.
Telescoping effect	The tendency to displace recent events backward in time and remote events forward in time, so that recent events appear more remote, and remote events, more recent.
Testing effect	The fact that you more easily remember information you have read by rewriting it instead of rereading it.[103]
Tip of the tongue phenomenon	When a subject is able to recall parts of an item, or related information, but is frustratingly unable to recall the whole item. This is thought an instance of "blocking" where multiple similar memories are being recalled and interfere with each other.[82]
Verbatim effect	That the "gist" of what someone has said is better remembered than the verbatim wording.[104] This is because memories are representations, not exact copies.

Von Restorff effect	That an item that sticks out is more likely to be remembered than other items[105]
Zeigarnik effect	That uncompleted or interrupted tasks are remembered better than completed ones.

Common theoretical causes of some cognitive biases

- **Bounded rationality** – limits on optimization and rationality

  o **Prospect theory**

  o **Mental accounting**

  o **Adaptive bias** – basing decisions on limited information and biasing them based on the costs of being wrong.

- **Attribute substitution** – making a complex, difficult judgment by unconsciously substituting it by an easier judgment[106]

- **Attribution theory**

  o **Salience**

  o **Naïve realism**

- **Cognitive dissonance**, and related:

  o **Impression management**

  o **Self-perception theory**

- **Heuristics in judgment and decision making**, including:

  o **Availability heuristic** – estimating what is more likely by what is more available in memory, which is biased toward vivid, unusual, or emotionally charged examples[47]

  o **Representativeness heuristic** – judging probabilities on the basis of resemblance[47]

72

- o **Affect heuristic** – basing a decision on an emotional reaction rather than a calculation of risks and benefits[107]

- Some theories of emotion such as:

  - o **Two-factor theory of emotion**

  - o **Somatic markers hypothesis**

- **Introspection illusion**

- Misinterpretations or **misuse of statistics**; **innumeracy**.

A 2012 *Psychological Bulletin* article suggested that at least eight seemingly unrelated biases can be produced by the same information-theoretic generative mechanism that assumes noisy information processing during storage and retrieval of information in human memory.[23]

See also

- Affective forecasting

- Apophenia

- Black swan theory

- Chronostasis

- Cognitive bias mitigation

- Cognitive distortion

- Cross-race effect

- Dysrationalia

- Frame rate

- List of common misconceptions

- List of fallacies

- List of memory biases

- Lists of thinking-related topics

- List of topics related to public relations and propaganda

- Logical fallacy

- Media bias

- Pareidolia

- Publication bias

- Recall bias

- Raster scan

- Saccade

- Saccadic masking

- Saccadic suppression of image displacement

- Systematic bias

- Transsaccadic memory

- Ψ **Psychology portal**

- **Sociology portal**

- **Thinking portal**

- **Logic portal**

Notes

1. Dougherty, M. R. P.; Gettys, C. F.; Ogden, E. E. (1999). "MINERVA-DM: A memory processes model for

74

judgments of likelihood". *Psychological Review* **106** (1): 180–209. doi:10.1037/0033-295x.106.1.180.

2. Kahneman, D.; Tversky, A. (1972). "Subjective probability: A judgment of representativeness". *Cognitive Psychology* **3**: 430–454. doi:10.1016/0010-0285(72)90016-3.

3. Baron, J. (2007). *Thinking and deciding* (4th ed. ed.). New York City: Cambridge University Press. ISBN 9781139466028.

4. Maccoun, Robert J. (1998). "Biases in the interpretation and use of research results". *Annual Review of Psychology* **49**: 259–87. doi:10.1146/annurev.psych.49.1.259. PMID 15012470.

5. Nickerson, Raymond S. (1998). "Confirmation Bias: A Ubiquitous Phenomenon in Many Guises". *Review of General Psychology* (Educational Publishing Foundation) **2** (2): 175–220 [198]. doi:10.1037/1089-2680.2.2.175. ISSN 1089-2680.

6. Dardenne, Benoit; Leyens, Jacques-Philippe (1995). "Confirmation Bias as a Social Skill". *Personality and Social Psychology Bulletin* (Society for Personality and Social Psychology) **21** (11): 1229–1239. doi:10.1177/01461672952111011. ISSN 1552-7433.

7. Alexander, William H.; Brown, Joshua W. (1 June 2010). "Hyperbolically Discounted Temporal Difference Learning". *Neural Computation* **22** (6): 1511–1527. doi:10.1162/neco.2010.08-09-1080. PMC 3005720.

8. Baron 1994, p. 372

9. Zhang, Yu; Lewis, Mark; Pellon, Michael; Coleman, Phillip (2007). "A Preliminary Research on Modeling Cognitive Agents for Social Environments in Multi-Agent Systems". pp. 116–123.

10. Iverson, Grant; Brooks, Brian; Holdnack, James (2008). "Misdiagnosis of Cognitive Impairment in Forensic Neuropsychology". In Heilbronner, Robert L. *Neuropsychology in the Courtroom: Expert Analysis of Reports and Testimony*. New York: Guilford Press. p. 248. ISBN 9781593856342.

11. (Bar-Haim, Y., Lamy, D., Pergamin, L., Bakermans-Kranenburg, M.J., & van IJzendoorn, M.H. (2007). Threat-related attentional bias in anxious and non-anxious individuals: A meta-analytic study. Psychological Bulletin.

12. Schwarz, N.; Bless, Herbert; Strack, Fritz; Klumpp, G.; Rittenauer-Schatka, Helga; Simons, Annette (1991). "Ease of Retrieval as Information: Another Look at the Availability Heuristic" (PDF). *Journal of Personality and Social Psychology* **61** (2): 195–202. doi:10.1037/0022-3514.61.2.195. Retrieved 19 Oct 2014.

13. Kuran, Timur; Cass R Sunstein (1998). "Availability Cascades and Risk Regulation". *Stanford Law Review* **51**: 683. doi:10.2307/1229439.

14. Sanna, Lawrence J.; Schwarz, Norbert; Stocker, Shevaun L. (2002). "When debiasing backfires: Accessible content and accessibility experiences in debiasing hindsight.". *Journal of Experimental Psychology: Learning, Memory, and Cognition* **28** (3): 497–502. doi:10.1037//0278-7393.28.3.497. ISSN 0278-7393.

15. Colman, Andrew (2003). *Oxford Dictionary of Psychology*. New York: Oxford University Press. p. 77. ISBN 0-19-280632-7.

16. Baron 1994, pp. 224–228

17. Klauer, K. C.; Musch, J; Naumer, B (2000). "On belief bias in syllogistic reasoning". *Psychological Review* **107** (4): 852–884. doi:10.1037/0033-295X.107.4.852. PMID 11089409.

18. Pronin, Emily; Matthew B. Kugler (July 2007). "Valuing thoughts, ignoring behavior: The introspection illusion as a source of the bias blind spot". *Journal of Experimental Social Psychology* (Elsevier) **43** (4): 565–578. doi:10.1016/j.jesp.2006.05.011. ISSN 0022-1031.

19. Walker, Drew; Vul, Edward (2013-10-25). "Hierarchical Encoding Makes Individuals in a Group Seem More Attractive". *Psychological Science* **20** (11). doi:10.1177/0956797613497969.

20. Mather, M.; Shafir, E.; Johnson, M.K. (2000). "Misrememberance of options past: Source monitoring and choice". *Psychological Science* **11** (2): 132–138. doi:10.1111/1467-9280.00228. PMID 11273420.

21. Oswald, Margit E.; Grosjean, Stefan (2004). "Confirmation Bias". In Pohl, Rüdiger F. *Cognitive Illusions: A Handbook on Fallacies and Biases in Thinking, Judgement and Memory*. Hove, UK: Psychology Press. pp. 79–96. ISBN 978-1-84169-351-4. OCLC 55124398.

22. Fisk, John E. (2004). "Conjunction fallacy". In Pohl, Rüdiger F. *Cognitive Illusions: A Handbook on Fallacies and Biases in Thinking, Judgement and Memory*. Hove,

UK: Psychology Press. pp. 23–42. ISBN 978-1-84169-351-4. OCLC 55124398.

23. Martin Hilbert (2012) ""Toward a synthesis of cognitive biases: How noisy information processing can bias human decision making"". *Psychological Bulletin*, 138(2), 211–237; Also at http://www.martinhilbert.net/HilbertPsychBull.pdf

24. Attneave, F. (1953). "Psychological probability as a function of experienced frequency". *Journal of Experimental Psychology* **46** (2): 81–86. doi:10.1037/h0057955. PMID 13084849.

25. Fischhoff, B.; Slovic, P.; Lichtenstein, S. (1977). "Knowing with certainty: The appropriateness of extreme confidence". *Journal of Experimental Psychology: Human Perception and Performance* **3** (4): 552–564. doi:10.1037/0096-1523.3.4.552.

26. DuCharme, W. M. (1970). "Response bias explanation of conservative human inference". *Journal of Experimental Psychology* **85** (1): 66–74. doi:10.1037/h0029546.

27. Edwards, W. (1968). "Conservatism in human information processing". In Kleinmuntz, B. *Formal representation of human judgment*. New York: Wiley. pp. 17–52.

28. Plous 1993, pp. 38–41

29. Ackerman, Mark S., ed. (2003). *Sharing expertise beyond knowledge management* (online ed.). Cambridge, Massachusetts: MIT Press. p. 7. ISBN 9780262011952.

30. Why We Spend Coins Faster Than Bills by Chana Joffe-Walt. All Things Considered, 12 May 2009.

31. Hsee, Christopher K.; Zhang, Jiao (2004). "Distinction bias: Misprediction and mischoice due to joint evaluation". *Journal of Personality and Social Psychology* **86** (5): 680–695. doi:10.1037/0022-3514.86.5.680. PMID 15161394.

32. (Kahneman, Knetsch & Thaler 1991, p. 193) Richard Thaler coined the term "endowment effect."

33. [1]

34. Wagenaar, W. A.; Keren, G. B. (1985). "Calibration of probability assessments by professional blackjack dealers, statistical experts, and lay people". *Organizational Behavior and Human Decision Processes* **36** (3): 406–416. doi:10.1016/0749-5978(85)90008-1.

35. Jeng, M. (2006). "A selected history of expectation bias in physics". *American Journal of Physics* **74** (7): 578–583. doi:10.1119/1.2186333.

36. Kahneman, Daniel; Alan B. Krueger; David Schkade; Norbert Schwarz; Arthur A. Stone (2006-06-30). "Would you be happier if you were richer? A focusing illusion". *Science* **312** (5782): 1908–10. doi:10.1126/science.1129688. PMID 16809528.

37. Zwicky, Arnold (2005-08-07). "Just Between Dr. Language and I". *Language Log*.

38. "There's a Name for That: The Baader-Meinhof Phenomenon".

39. Lichtenstein, S., & Fischhoff, B. (1977). Do those who know more also know more about how much they know? Organizational Behavior and Human Performance, 20(2), 159–183. doi:10.1016/0030-5073(77)90001-0

40. Merkle, E. C. (2009). "The disutility of the hard-easy effect in choice confidence". *Psychonomic Bulletin & Review* **16** (1): 204–213. doi:10.3758/PBR.16.1.204.

41. Juslin, P; Winman, A.; Olsson, H. (2000). "Naive empiricism and dogmatism in confidence research: a critical examination of the hard-easy effect". *Psychological Review* **107** (2): 384–396. doi:10.1037/0033-295x.107.2.384.

42. Pohl, Rüdiger F. (2004). "Hindsight Bias". In Pohl, Rüdiger F. *Cognitive Illusions: A Handbook on Fallacies and Biases in Thinking, Judgement and Memory*. Hove, UK: Psychology Press. pp. 363–378. ISBN 978-1-84169-351-4. OCLC 55124398.

43. Laibson, David (1997). "Golden Eggs and Hyperbolic Discounting". *Quarterly Journal of Economics* **112** (2): 443–477. doi:10.1162/003355397555253.

44. Kogut, Tehila; Ritov, Ilana (2005). "The 'Identified Victim' Effect: An Identified Group, or Just a Single Individual?". *Journal of Behavioral Decision Making* (Wiley InterScience) **18**: 157–167. doi:10.1002/bdm.492. Retrieved August 15, 2013.

45. Thompson, Suzanne C. (1999). "Illusions of Control: How We Overestimate Our Personal Influence". *Current Directions in Psychological Science* (Association for Psychological Science) **8** (6): 187–190. doi:10.1111/1467-8721.00044. ISSN 0963-7214. JSTOR 20182602.

46. Dierkes, Meinolf; Antal, Ariane Berthoin; Child, John; Ikujiro Nonaka (2003). *Handbook of Organizational Learning and Knowledge*. Oxford University Press. p. 22. ISBN 978-0-19-829582-2. Retrieved 9 September

2013.http://books.google.se/books?id=JRd7RZzzw_wC&pg=PA22&dq=Illusion+of+validity&hl=en&sa=X&ei=lr4tUoKtOKKK4wSi3IEw&redir_esc=y#v=onepage&q=Illusion%20of%20validity&f=false

47. Tversky, Amos; Daniel Kahneman (September 27, 1974). "Judgment under Uncertainty: Heuristics and Biases". *Science* (American Association for the Advancement of Science) **185** (4157): 1124–1131. doi:10.1126/science.185.4157.1124. PMID 17835457.

48. Fiedler, K. (1991). "The tricky nature of skewed frequency tables: An information loss account of distinctiveness-based illusory correlations". *Journal of Personality and Social Psychology* **60** (1): 24–36. doi:10.1037/0022-3514.60.1.24.

49. Sanna, Lawrence J.; Schwarz, Norbert (2004). "Integrating Temporal Biases: The Interplay of Focal Thoughts and Accessibility Experiences". *Psychological Science* (American Psychological Society) **15** (7): 474–481. doi:10.1111/j.0956-7976.2004.00704.x. PMID 15200632.

50. Baron 1994, pp. 258–259

51. (Kahneman, Knetsch & Thaler 1991, p. 193) Daniel Kahneman, together with Amos Tversky, coined the term "loss aversion."

52. Bornstein, Robert F.; Crave-Lemley, Catherine (2004). "Mere exposure effect". In Pohl, Rüdiger F. *Cognitive Illusions: A Handbook on Fallacies and Biases in Thinking, Judgement and Memory*. Hove, UK: Psychology Press. pp. 215–234. ISBN 978-1-84169-351-4. OCLC 55124398.

53. Shafir, Eldar; Diamond, Peter; Tversky, Amos (2000). "Money Illusion". In Kahneman, Daniel; Tversky, Amos.

Choices, values, and frames. Cambridge University Press. pp. 335–355. ISBN 978-0-521-62749-8.

54. Haizlip, Julie et al. "Perspective: The Negativity Bias, Medical Education, and the Culture of Academic Medicine: Why Culture Change Is Hard". Retrieved October 3, 2012.

55. Baron 1994, p. 353

56. Baron 1994, p. 386

57. Baron 1994, p. 44

58. Hardman 2009, p. 104

59. Adams, P. A., & Adams, J. K. (1960). Confidence in the recognition and reproduction of words difficult to spell. The American Journal of Psychology, 73(4), 544–552.

60. Hoffrage, Ulrich (2004). "Overconfidence". In Rüdiger Pohl. *Cognitive Illusions: a handbook on fallacies and biases in thinking, judgement and memory*. Psychology Press. ISBN 978-1-84169-351-4.

61. Sutherland 2007, pp. 172–178

62. Hardman 2009, p. 137

63. Garcia, Stephen M.; Song, Hyunjin; Tesser, Abraham (November 2010). "Tainted recommendations: The social comparison bias". *Organizational Behavior and Human Decision Processes* **113** (2): 97–101. doi:10.1016/j.obhdp.2010.06.002. ISSN 0749-5978. Lay summary – *BPS Research Digest* (2010-10-30).

64. Dalton, D. & Ortegren, M. (2011). "Gender differences in ethics research: The importance of controlling for the social

desirability response bias". *Journal of Business Ethics* **103** (1): 73–93. doi:10.1007/s10551-011-0843-8.

65. Kahneman, Knetsch & Thaler 1991, p. 193

66. Baron 1994, p. 382

67. Baron, J. (in preparation). *Thinking and Deciding*, 4th edition. New York: Cambridge University Press.

68. "Penn Psychologists Believe 'Unit Bias' Determines The Acceptable Amount To Eat". ScienceDaily (Nov. 21, 2005)

69. Meegan, Daniel V. (2010). "Zero-Sum Bias: Perceived Competition Despite Unlimited Resources". *Frontiers in Psychology* **1**. doi:10.3389/fpsyg.2010.00191. ISSN 1664-1078.

70. Chernev, Alexander (2007). "Jack of All Trades or Master of One? Product Differentiation and Compensatory Reasoning in Consumer Choice". *Journal of Consumer Research* **33** (4): 430–444. doi:10.1086/510217. ISSN 0093-5301.

71. Morris, Errol (2010-06-20). "The Anosognosic's Dilemma: Something's Wrong but You'll Never Know What It Is (Part 1)". *Opinionator: Exclusive Online Commentary from the* New York Times. New York Times. Retrieved 2011-03-07.

72. Marks, Gary; Miller, Norman (1987). "Ten years of research on the false-consensus effect: An empirical and theoretical review". *Psychological Bulletin* (American Psychological Association) **102** (1): 72–90. doi:10.1037/0033-2909.102.1.72.

73. Sutherland 2007, pp. 138–139

74. Baron 1994, p. 275

75. Pronin, E.; Kruger, J.; Savitsky, K.; Ross, L. (2001). "You don't know me, but I know you: the illusion of asymmetric insight". *Journal of Personality and Social Psychology* **81** (4): 639–656. doi:10.1037/0022-3514.81.4.639. PMID 11642351.

76. Hoorens, Vera (1993). "Self-enhancement and Superiority Biases in Social Comparison". *European Review of Social Psychology* (Psychology Press) **4** (1): 113–139. doi:10.1080/14792779343000040.

77. Plous 2006, p. 206

78. Hsee, Christopher K.; Hastie, Reid (2006). "Decision and experience: why don't we choose what makes us happy?". *Trends in Cognitive Sciences* **10** (1): 31–37. doi:10.1016/j.tics.2005.11.007. PMID 16318925.

79. Plous 2006, p. 185

80. Forsyth, D. R. (2009). *Group Dynamics* (5th ed.). Pacific Grove, CA: Brooks/Cole.

81. Kruger, J. (1999). "Lake Wobegon be gone! The "below-average effect" and the egocentric nature of comparative ability judgments". *Journal of Personality and Social Psychology* **77** (2): 221–32. doi:10.1037/0022-3514.77.2.221. PMID 10474208.

82. Schacter, Daniel L. (1999). "The Seven Sins of Memory: Insights From Psychology and Cognitive Neuroscience". *American Psychologist* **54** (3): 182–203. doi:10.1037/0003-066X.54.3.182. PMID 10199218.

83. Cacioppo, John (2002). *Foundations in social neuroscience*. Cambridge, Mass: MIT Press. pp. 130–132. ISBN 026253195X.

84. Walker, W. Richard; John J. Skowronski; Charles P. Thompson (2003). "Life Is Pleasant—and Memory Helps to Keep It That Way!". *Review of General Psychology* (Educational Publishing Foundation) **7** (2): 203–210. doi:10.1037/1089-2680.7.2.203. Retrieved 2009-08-27.

85. Koriat, A.; M. Goldsmith; A. Pansky (2000). "Toward a Psychology of Memory Accuracy". *Annual Review of Psychology* **51** (1): 481–537. doi:10.1146/annurev.psych.51.1.481. PMID 10751979.

86. Craik & Lockhart, 1972

87. Kinnell, Angela; Dennis, S. (2011). "The list length effect in recognition memory: an analysis of potential confounds". *Memory & Cognition* (Adelaide, Australia: School of Psychology, University of Adelaide) **39** (2): 348–63. doi:10.3758/s13421-010-0007-6.

88. Wayne Weiten (2010). *Psychology: Themes and Variations: Themes and Variations*. Cengage Learning. p. 338. ISBN 978-0-495-60197-5.

89. Wayne Weiten (2007). *Psychology: Themes and Variations: Themes And Variations*. Cengage Learning. p. 260. ISBN 978-0-495-09303-9.

90. Slamecka NJ (1968). "An examination of trace storage in free recall". *J Exp Psychol* **76** (4): 504–13. doi:10.1037/h0025695. PMID 5650563.

91. Shepard, R.N. (1967). Recognition memory for words, sentences, and pictures. *Journal of Learning and Verbal Behavior* 6, 156–163.

92. McBride, D. M.; Dosher, B.A. (2002). "A comparison of conscious and automatic memory processes for picture and word stimuli: a process dissociation analysis". *Consciousness and Cognition* **11**: 423–460. doi:10.1016/s1053-8100(02)00007-7.

93. Defetyer, M. A., Russo, R., McPartlin, P. L. (2009). The picture superiority effect in recognition memory: a developmental study using the response signal procedure. *Cognitive Development* 24, 265–273. doi:10.1016/j.cogdev.2009.05.002

94. Whitehouse, A. J., Maybery, M.T., Durkin, K. (2006). The development of the picture-superiority effect. *British Journal of Developmental Psychology* 24, 767–773. doi:10.1348/026151005X74153

95. Ally, B. A.; Gold, C. A.; Budson, A. E. (2009). "The picture superiority effect in patients with Alzheimer's disease and mild cognitive impairment". *Neuropsychologia* **47**: 595–598. doi:10.1016/j.neuropsychologia.2008.10.010.

96. Curran, T.; Doyle, J. (2011). "Picture superiority doubly dissociates the ERP correlates of recollection and familiarity". *Journal of Cognitive Neuroscience* **23** (5): 1247–1262. doi:10.1162/jocn.2010.21464.

97. Martin, G. Neil; Neil R. Carlson; William Buskist (2007). *Psychology* (3rd ed.). Pearson Education. pp. 309–310. ISBN 978-0-273-71086-8.

98. "When comprehension difficulty improves memory for text." O'Brien, Edward J.; Myers, Jerome L. *Journal of*

Experimental Psychology: Learning, Memory, and Cognition, Vol 11(1), Jan 1985, 12–21. doi:10.1037/0278-7393.11.1.12

99. Rubin, Wetzler & Nebes, 1986; Rubin, Rahhal & Poon, 1998

100.   "A. Lieberman (8 December 2011). *Human Learning and Memory*. Cambridge University Press. p. 432. ISBN 978-1-139-50253-5.

101.   Morton, Crowder & Prussin, 1971

102.   Ian Pitt; Alistair D. N. Edwards (2003). *Design of Speech-Based Devices: A Practical Guide*. Springer. p. 26. ISBN 978-1-85233-436-9.

103.   E. Bruce Goldstein. *Cognitive Psychology: Connecting Mind, Research and Everyday Experience*. Cengage Learning. p. 231. ISBN 978-1-133-00912-2.

104.   Poppenk, Walia, Joanisse, Danckert, & Köhler, 2006

105.   Von Restorff, H (1933). "Über die Wirkung von Bereichsbildungen im Spurenfeld (The effects of field formation in the trace field)".". *Psychological Research* **18** (1): 299–342. doi:10.1007/bf02409636.

106.   Kahneman, Daniel; Shane Frederick (2002). "Representativeness Revisited: Attribute Substitution in Intuitive Judgment". In Thomas Gilovich, Dale Griffin, Daniel Kahneman. *Heuristics and Biases: The Psychology of Intuitive Judgment*. Cambridge: Cambridge University Press. pp. 49–81. ISBN 978-0-521-79679-8. OCLC 47364085.

107.   Slovic, Paul; Melissa Finucane; Ellen Peters; Donald G. MacGregor (2002). "The Affect Heuristic". In Thomas Gilovich, Dale Griffin, Daniel Kahneman. *Heuristics and Biases: The Psychology of Intuitive Judgment*. Cambridge University Press. pp. 397–420. ISBN 0-521-79679-2.